My Latter Days

Planner

Advanced Directive &
Last Will and Testament

Yamin

My Latter Days

Planner

Advanced Directive &
Last Will and Testament

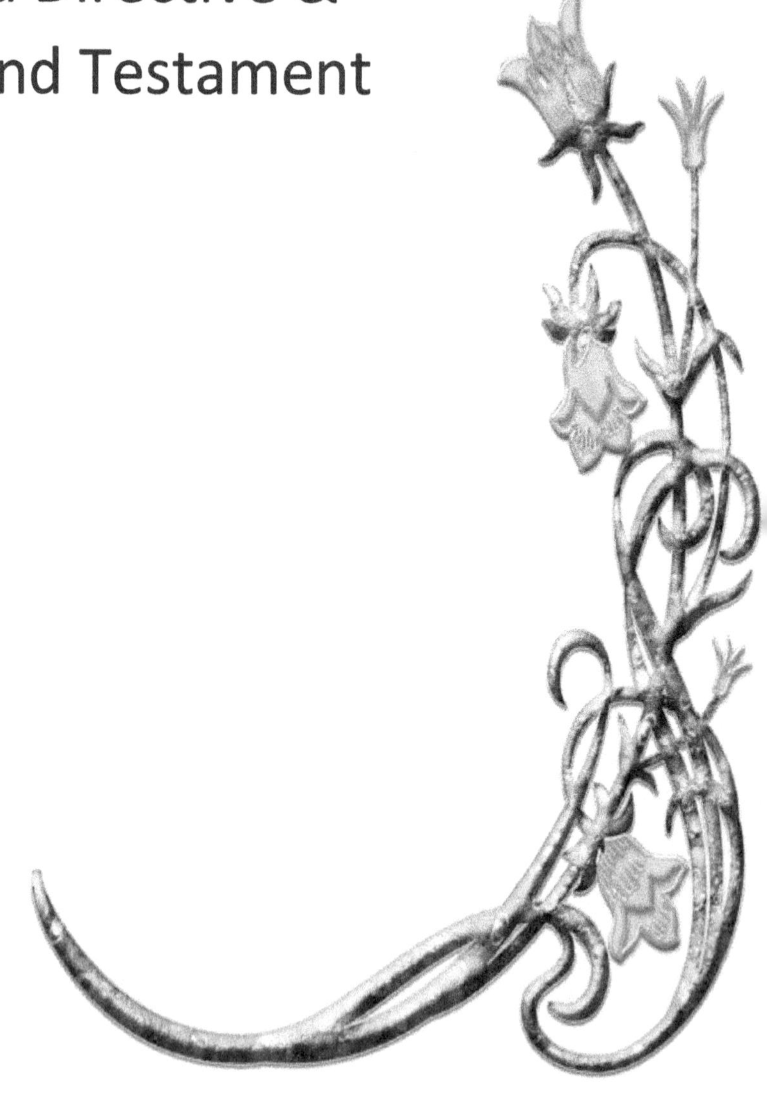

Framed by Time
By
Deborah Judge

Life's lessons can be costly, that's what my mom used to say. But I didn't pay much attention to those old sayings, because I liked doing things my way.

Time after time I would often hit a brick wall, I thought I knew exactly how to get the job done, I didn't need anyone's advice, because you know I knew it all.

Then there were those times when I would put things off, not realizing how much time that would be lost.

One day while looking at my hands I noticed some things, I ran to the mirror, and without makeup I was amazed at what I had seen. There were lines and wrinkles that were so profound, I let out a scream! I realized that my life was framed by time and time had created every wrinkle and every line.

Where did the time go? Have I put off so many things in life without detection, I was standing there trying to figure out how I lost my direction.

I must have gotten off track because of all of life's drama and people I carried on my back.

I begin to pray and ask my Father some questions, it had been a while since I asked him for answers.

He didn't answer me in the way I expected, He said I have given you many assignments and instructions, but it was "My" words you rejected.

You know daughter sometimes we are looking for someone else to blame. If you really want to know who is your worse enemy, just speak your name.

I hurried to my journal where I wrote many of His instructions down, you know write the vision and make it plain, but when I looked at the dates, 10 – 15 years had passed, and I became tearfully ashamed.

I picked myself up and wiped the tears from my face and then I repented to my Father and asked for more grace.

I went again to the mirror, this time looking beyond the image of my youth that time had erased, I looked in the mirror to make a declaration to myself, you know face to face.

I declare I will recognize my enemy, even if the enemy is me, I will focus and understand the assignment He has given me. I will remove all of the stumbling blocks so my pathway will be free.

 I will be determined to make it to the finish line. I am going to be about my Father's business, because now I know what it means to be framed by time.

Introduction

Life is a journey. Regardless of our expectations of how things should go, there are always bumps and potholes in the road. As we are going along the unexpected things happen. When that happens, we often times must regroup and face the challenges head on. We have prepared this planner to help families organize and prepare for the challenging decisions we all must make someday. An Advanced Directive is a written statement or statements of a person's wishes regarding medical treatment, often including a living will with personal instructions, made to ensure those wishes are carried out should the person be unable to communicate them to family or a doctor.

When a family member can no longer make sound decisions for their care, often times family members tend to be conflicted about what is the best decision for their loved one. This can get quite intense when everyone believes they have the right answer. The truth of the matter is only the person who is in crisis knows what they desire for themselves if this ever occurs in their lives.`

For an Advanced Directive and Will to be done in a most effective way, is to have these conversations while people are healthy enough to make sound decisions for their care. If they get to the point where they are unable to care for themselves, who will be assigned to care for them, take care of the finances, make medical decisions, end of life wishes, funeral instructions and so on.

There is a lot to be considered when we or our loved ones start aging or suffering from a terminal illness. Families tend to avoid these conversations. These conversations are difficult to have, especially when the reality of someone we love dearly may die and leave us forever. However, there is peace in knowing that when that time comes, our loved ones made the decision for themselves. When these things are not planned there is always the question, "Did I make the right decision?" Having these documents in place will also shut the mouth of those who cause discord among the family. You know the ones that claim that the deceased one left them everything or claim to know every wish the person wanted. When we carry out the last wishes of others, we are honoring their wishes and honoring who they were in our lives.

Advance Directive for the state of Texas. Remember each state has its own guidelines.

Guidelines for completing your TEXAS ADVANCE DIRECTIVE How do I make my Texas Advance Directive legal? The law requires that you sign your advance directive, or direct another to sign it, in the presence of two adult witnesses, who must also sign the document. At least one witness cannot be:
• the person you name as your agent,
• related to you by blood or marriage,
• your doctor or an employee of your doctor,
• an employee of a health care facility in which you are a patient (if he or she is involved in your care),
• if you are a patient or resident in a health care facility, an officer, director, partner, or business office employee of the health care facility or of any parent organization of the health care facility,
• a person entitled to any part of your estate upon your death either by will or operation of law, or
• any other person who has a claim against your estate at the time you sign the Medical Power of Attorney.

Whom should I appoint as my agent?
Your agent is the person you appoint to make decisions about your health care if you become unable to make those decisions yourself. Your agent may be a family member or a close friend whom you trust to make serious decisions. The person you name as your agent should clearly understand your wishes and be willing to accept the responsibility of making health care decisions for you. You can appoint a second person as your alternate agent. The alternate will step in if the first person you name as an agent is unable, unwilling, or unavailable to act for you.

The person you appoint as your agent cannot be:
• your doctor or other treating health care provider,
• an employee of your treating health care provider who is not related to you,
• your residential care provider, or
• an employee of your residential care provider who is not related to you.

Should I add personal instructions to my Texas Advance Directive?

One of the strongest reasons for naming an agent is to have someone who can respond flexibly as your health care situation changes and deal with situations that you did not foresee. If you add instructions to this document, it may help your agent carry out your wishes, but be careful that you do not unintentionally restrict your agent's power to act 5 in your best interest. In any event, be sure to talk with your agent about your future medical care and describe what you consider to be an acceptable "quality of life."

What if I change my mind?
You may revoke Part I, your Texas Medical Power of Attorney at any time by:
• notifying your agent, doctor, or residential care provider of your revocation (this may be done orally, in writing or by any other act which demonstrates your intent to revoke your agent's power); or
• executing another medical power of attorney. If you appoint your spouse as your agent, and your marriage is dissolved or annulled, your agent's authority is automatically revoked, unless your Texas Medical Power of Attorney provides otherwise.
You may revoke Part II, your Texas Directive at any time by:
• canceling, defacing, obliterating, burning, tearing, or otherwise destroying the directive, or by having someone destroy your directive at your direction and in your presence, or
• signing and dating a written revocation, or • orally stating your intent to revoke the directive. You or someone acting on your behalf must notify your doctor of the revocation. What other important facts should I know? Directions to withhold or withdraw life-sustaining treatments from a pregnant patient will not be given effect under Texas law. Your agent does not have the authority to consent to voluntary inpatient mental health services; convulsive treatment; psychosurgery; abortion; or your neglect through the omission of care primarily intended to provide for your comfort.

TEXAS ADVANCE DIRECTIVE – PAGE 1 OF 14 PART I: Medical Power of Attorney Disclosure Statement for Medical Power of Attorney INFORMATION CONCERNING THE MEDICAL POWER OF ATTORNEY THIS IS AN IMPORTANT LEGAL DOCUMENT. BEFORE SIGNING THIS DOCUMENT, YOU SHOULD KNOW THESE IMPORTANT FACTS: DISCLOSURE STATEMENT © 2005 National Hospice and Palliative Care Organization 2022 Revised. Except to the extent, you state otherwise, this document gives the person you name as your agent the authority to make all health care decisions for you in accordance with your wishes, including your religious and moral beliefs, when you are no longer capable of making them yourself. Because "health care" means any treatment, service, or procedure to maintain, diagnose, or treat your physical or mental condition, your agent has the power to make a broad range of health care decisions for you. Your agent may consent, refuse to consent, or withdraw consent to medical treatment and may make decisions about withdrawing or withholding life-sustaining treatment. Your agent may not consent to voluntary inpatient mental health services, convulsive treatment, psychosurgery, or abortion. A physician must comply with your agent's instructions or allow you to be transferred to another physician.

Your agent's authority begins when your doctor certifies that you lack the competence to make health care decisions. Your agent is obligated to follow your instructions when making decisions on your behalf. Unless you state otherwise, your agent has the same authority to make decisions about your health care as you would have had. It is important that you discuss this document with your physician or other health care provider before you sign it to make sure that you understand the nature and range of decisions that may be made on your behalf. If you do not have a physician, you should talk with someone else who is knowledgeable about these issues and can answer your questions.

You do not need a lawyer's assistance to complete this document, but if there is anything in this document that you do not understand, you should ask a lawyer to explain it to you. The person you appoint as agent should be someone you know and trust. The person must be 18 years of age or older or a person under 18 years of age who has had the disabilities of minority removed. If you appoint your health or residential care provider (e.g., your physician or an employee of a home health agency, hospital, nursing home, or residential care home, other than a relative), that person has to choose between 7 TEXAS ADVANCE DIRECTIVE – PAGE 2 OF 14 acting as your agent or as your health or residential care provider; the law does not permit a person to do both at the same time. You should inform the person you appoint that you want the person to be your health care agent. You should discuss this document with your agent and your physician and give each a signed copy. You should indicate on the document itself the people and institutions who have signed copies. Your agent is not liable for healthcare decisions made in good faith on your behalf. DISCLOSURE STATEMENT (CONTINUED) © 2005 National Hospice and

Palliative Care Organization 2022 Revised. Even after you have signed this document, you have the right to make health care decisions for yourself as long as you are able to do so, and treatment cannot be given to you or stopped over your objection. You have the right to revoke the authority granted to your agent by informing your agent or your health or residential care provider orally or in writing, or by your execution of a subsequent medical power of attorney. Unless you state otherwise, your appointment of a spouse dissolves on divorce. This document may not be changed or modified. If you want to make changes to the document, you must make an entirely new one. You may wish to designate an alternate agent in the event that your agent is unwilling, unable, or ineligible to act as your agent. Any alternate agent you designate has the same authority to make health care decisions for you.

THIS POWER OF ATTORNEY IS NOT VALID UNLESS: (1) YOU SIGN IT AND HAVE YOUR SIGNATURE ACKNOWLEDGED BEFORE A NOTARY PUBLIC; OR (2) YOU SIGN IT IN THE PRESENCE OF TWO COMPETENT ADULT WITNESSES. THE FOLLOWING PERSONS MAY NOT ACT AS ONE OF THE WITNESSES: (1) the person you have designated as your agent; (2) a person related to you by blood or marriage; (3) a person entitled to any part of your estate after your death under a will or codicil executed by you or by operation of law; (4) your attending physician; (5) an employee of your attending physician; 8 TEXAS ADVANCE DIRECTIVE – PAGE 3 OF 14 (6) an employee of your health care facility in which you are a patient if the employee is providing direct patient care to you or is an officer, director, partner, or business office employee of the health care facility or of any parent organization of the health care facility; or (7) a person who, at the time this power of attorney is executed, has a claim against any part of your estate after your death. IF YOU PLAN TO DESIGNATE AN AGENT IN PART I, YOU MUST READ AND UNDERSTAND THE DISCLOSURE STATEMENT AND SIGN AND DATE HERE BEFORE EXECUTING YOUR ADVANCE DIRECTIVE © 2005 National Hospice and Palliative Care Organization 2022 Revised.

Acknowledgement of Disclosure Statement I am signing this acknowledgement that I have received, read, and understand the above disclosure statement prior to executing the medical power of attorney in this document.
Signature ____ Date ___________________

Advanced Directive Examples

TO MY FAMILY, FRIENDSAND HEALTH-CARE PROVIDERS

1. I, ____ .
   [Print your full name here]

   of ____ ,
   [Print here the number of your house, name of your street and suburb]

   State: _________________________   Postcode: _________________ .
   [Print here the name of the State where you live]

   born on ____ .
   [Print here the date of your birth]

being over the age of eighteen years, make this directive after careful consideration and of my own free will.

If at any time I am unable to take part in decisions about my medical care, let this document stand as evidence of my views, wishes and beliefs about my quality of life and the medical treatment I require.

This directive should never be used if I have the capacity to speak competently for myself or if there is evidence that it has been revoked.

I sign this document in the full knowledge that my health care may be limited as a result, but only as specified below.

I request that all who are responsible for my care respect the directions given in this document.

Advance Directive

MY NAME .... DATE OF BIRTH .... DATE SIGNED. ....

ADDRESS ..... ⬜ ....

CITY ..⬜ .... STATE .... ZIP. ....

PHONE .... EMAIL..

1. I want my agent to make decisions for me: (choose one statement below*)
    _____ when I am no longer able to make health care decisions for myself, or
    _____ immediately, allowing my agent to make decisions for me right now, or
    _____ when the following condition or event occurs (to be determined as follows):
    ____

    Normally these statements are separate choices, but it is conceivable that they could be concurrent.

2. I appoint _____________________ as my health care Agent to make any and all health care decisions for me, except to the extent that I state otherwise in this Advance Directive. (You may cross out the italicized phrase if authority is unrestricted.)
    Address: ____
    Relationship (optional): ____
    Tel. (daytime): ___________________ (evening): _________________________
    cellphone: _______________________ email: _____________________________

3. If this health care agent is unavailable, unable or unwilling to do this for me, I appoint ____ to be my Alternate Agent.
    Address: ____
    Relationship (optional): ____
    Tel. (daytime): ___________________ (evening): _________________________
    cellphone: _______________________ email: _____________________________

    And if my Alternate Agent is unavailable, unable or unwilling to do this, I appoint ____ as my Next Alternate Agent.
    Address: ____
    Relationship (optional): ____
    Tel. (daytime): ___________________ (evening): _________________________
    cellphone: _______________________ email: _____________________________

Choosing an agent: Fill in your name and the name of the person you choose to be your agent to make health care decisions for you here:

My name____

My agent's name____

Title or relationship to me____

My agent's address____

My agent's home phone (___)__________________ My agent's work phone (___)________________

If the agent I have named above is not willing, reasonably available or able to make decisions for me, I choose the following person to be my agent:

If the person I have named as Choice # 2 is not willing, reasonably available or able to make decisions for me, I choose the following person to be my agent:

<u>Choice # 2 to be my agent</u>

Name_______________________________________

Title or Relationship to me__________________

Address____________________________________

____

Home Phone (___)___________________________

Work Phone (___)___________________________

<u>Choice # 3 to be my agent</u>

Name_______________________________________

Title or Relationship to me__________________

Address____________________________________

____

Home Phone (___)___________________________

Work Phone (___)___________________________

You may change your mind later about who you want to be your agent. If you want to stop the agent you have named from making decisions for you, you must tell your primary physician or fill in these blanks:

I do **not** want ___________________ to be my agent. ___________________________________
                                                                                                      My signature

Date you filled out and signed this section ___________________

Any time you cancel, replace or change this form you should give copies of the changed or new form to everyone who has a copy of your original form.

ADVANCE DIRECTIVE FOR HEALTH CARE

YOUR NAME _________________________________ DATE OF BIRTH ___________ DATE _______________

ADDRESS ____

CITY _______________________________________ STATE _______________ ZIP _______________

PART ONE: YOUR HEALTH CARE AGENT

Your health care agent can make health care decisions for you when you are unable or unwilling to make decisions for yourself. You should pick someone that you trust, who understands your wishes and *agrees* to act as your agent.

I appoint this person to be my health care AGENT:

NAME ____

ADDRESS ____

HOME PHONE _______________________________ WORK PHONE _______________________________

CELL PHONE ________________________________ EMAIL _____________________________________

(If you appoint co-agents, list them above or on a separate sheet of paper)

If this agent is unavailable, unwilling or unable to act as my agent, I appoint this person as my **alternate agent:**

NAME ____

ADDRESS: ____

HOME PHONE _______________________________ WORK PHONE _______________________________

CELL PHONE ________________________________ EMAIL _____________________________________

Others who can be consulted about medical decisions on my behalf include:

Primary care provider(s):

NAME _______________________________________ PHONE _______________________________

ADDRESS ____

NAME _______________________________________ PHONE _______________________________

ADDRESS ____

Last Will and Testament

A last will and testament is a legal document that communicates a person's final wishes pertaining to all of their assets. It provides specific instructions about what to do with their possessions. It will indicate whether the deceased leaves them to another person, a group, or wishes to donate them to charity.

A last will and testament can also oversee matters involving dependents, pets and even plants. It also instructs how the management of accounts and financial interests are handled.

Some states allow for non-standard or unusual wills, such as a video and holographic wills, while others do not. If you decide to create a non-traditional will, first check with your state to see if it will be recognized.

Things to Consider:

A will and last testament directs the disposition of your assets, such as bank balances, property, or prized possessions. It will detail who is to receive property and for what amount. It can establish guardian arrangements for surviving dependents.

- Having a last will and testament gives you some control over what happens to your assets after your death. Whether you have a little or a lot. A will can eliminate stress and confusion for family and friends.
- If you die without a will, your estate, including the distribution of all assets, is settled by the courts. Often family members, friends, and business partners are feuding over who your assets should go to. For instance: " Mama left that to me." "Granddad told me everything was going to me." This often happens when there is no will in place.
- If parents with children die without a will, the courts will appoint a guardian for those who are minors. It is important to designate someone you trust with the future of your children.
- Trusts and financial accounts. including life insurance policies, with named beneficiaries do not pass through probate court.
- Today, wills can be drafted online, or you can purchase software.

Writing Your Own Will

With some careful planning and preparation, it is entirely possible to write your own will. This is a simple way of doing it and it can be handwritten, typed or video. Check with your state to see what is acceptable.

(Please note that this list assumes you have a simple and straightforward estate and consequently want to write a simple will. If you have a complex or large estate involving many moving parts, this guide may not be useful to you. Consider instead the benefits of hiring an estate attorney.)

Suggested Information to include:

1. **Write a title.** It is easy to overlook such a simple detail, but it needs to be clear to anyone who picks up this document that it is your last will and testament. Make sure you include your full legal name somewhere near the beginning of your will. " Last Will and Testament of (your Name). If you have made previous versions of your will, be sure to also mention that your most current document invalidates any previous ones. Include any other names you have used.

2. **Name the executor of your will.** This is the person responsible for making sure your estate is distributed and settled according to your will. Choose someone you trust. Also consider choosing a 2nd and 3rd executor as a backup, life happens, and it is always good to have a backup plan.

3. **Name a guardian for any minors.** If you have children or are the guardian of any minors, name a guardian. This person takes full legal and physical custody of your children after your death. Guardianship typically passes automatically to any surviving parent as long as the parent can be deemed competent. If your children have Godparents, you need to name them in the will if your desire is for them to become their guardian. Have this discussion with them before including them in the will, over time many things change in relationships. You want to have a 2nd choice listed as a safety precaution.

4. Also consider guardianship of any pets.

5. **Organize and inventory assets.** Assets are any possessions clearly belonging to you or that are titled in your name. Personal belongings, pets, property, and cash are all considered your assets. Take the time to clearly describe each asset such that when the executor is transferring the asset to its named beneficiary there is no question about its identity. Be sure to check with your state about which assets you cannot include. Trusts or investment accounts, for example, are often not considered part of your simple assets and pass directly to the beneficiaries you have named on those accounts.

6. **Name the beneficiaries.** For each asset, name a beneficiary—the person, profit or non-profit organization or other entity to receive your asset(s) once you pass. You can choose one or many. If there is anyone who should not receive the asset in question, be sure to name them as well.

7. **Write your residuary clause.** A residuary clause covers everything not left to a specific beneficiary and either not adequately described or anything forgotten when you write the assets section of the will. You can choose to leave these "remainders" to a beneficiary or leave it to your executor to handle. Do not overlook the importance of this clause; it is unlikely you will remember everything you own, especially if this is your first pass at will. Having a residuary clause is a decent enough fail-safe to let you sleep at night. Example: Pictures, dishes, linen and so on.

8. **Sign your will with witnesses.** Check with your state requirements before signing, as different states have varying requirements regarding the number and identity of witnesses. Some states may also require you to have your will notarized. No will is legally valid until it has been signed before witnesses.

9. **Store your will someplace safe and update it when necessary.** Say someone named in the will dies or becomes unable to make sound decisions. Make these changes as quickly as possible. Let somebody—usually your executor—know where to find the most recent copy of your will. You may want to mail a copy to yourself and sign it with do not open until after my death and put in a safe place. Be sure to revisit and update

it whenever you experience a big life change: moving (especially because your will may not meet the laws in your new state or country), a large purchase or property investment, a change in your business, a marriage, divorce or death and even your children reaching adult age are all occasions to review your will.

You also might want to consider a Medical/General Power of Attorney. This is another option of having someone appointed to handle your business if you become unable to make decisions for yourself. Contact your state to explore your options.

It may also be a good idea to set aside a regular time, perhaps every other year or so, where you review your will even if no big changes have happened in your life. You may be surprised at what assets you consider important enough to describe two years in the future. Likewise, your opinions on beneficiaries and desires regarding asset division may change. Wills are not comfortable to write, but necessary to do for your peace of mind. Knowing you are making the best decisions for your loved ones.

Examples of Last Will and Testaments

LAST WILL AND TESTAMENT OF

____

I, _____________________, a resident of _____________, County, within the State of Georgia, make, publish and declare this to be my Last Will and Testament, revoking all Wills and Codicils previously made by me.

ARTICLE 1: BACKGROUND

1.1   I am married to _______________, divorced from _____________, separated from _______________________, widowed   from   _____________________,   engaged   to _______________, not married.

1.2   My _______________ and I have _________________________ children. The names and birth dates of each of our children are: _____________________________. All references in this Will to my "child" or "children" are to these named children as well as any child subsequently born to or adopted by me.

_(Or)_

1.3   I have ___________________________________ children. The names and birth dates of each of my children are: _______________________________. All references in this Will to my "child" or "children" are to these children as well as any child subsequently born to or adopted by me.

_(Or)_

1.4   I have no Descendants

1.5   All references in this Will to the Descendants of any person shall mean their naturally born children and legally adopted children less than 18 years of age (unless indicated otherwise) as well as any of their children's naturally born children and legally adopted children less than 18 years of age throughout the generations to come.

ARTICLE 2: BURIAL

2.1   I request that my Executor make arrangements for funeral services to be conducted at _______________________________ followed by a memorial service to be held at

_______________________________.

2.2   I request that my Executor make arrangements for my remains be buried at _______________________________;   cremated   with   the   ashes   given   to _______________________________;   cremated   with   the   ashes   deposited   at _______________________;   with   a   suitable   memorial   erected   at

_______________________________.

2.3   All costs and expenses associated with these requests shall be paid from my estate.

LAST WILL AND TESTAMENT
OF

____

I, ____, residing at ___________________________________, City
___________________________________, County ___________________________________, in the State of
___________________________________, being of sound mind and memory do hereby revoke any and all former Wills,
Testament and Codicils and declare this to be my Last Will and Testament.

I bear witness that there is no deity worthy of worship except Allah, and Prophet Muhammad, may peace and
blessing be upon him, is His Servant and last Messenger. I ask my relatives and friends, whether they believe as
I believe or not, to honor my right to these beliefs. I ask them to honor this document and not to obstruct it or
change it in any way. Rather, let them see that I am buried as I ask and let my properties be divided as I express
in this document.

Article I. FUNERAL AND BURIAL RITES

I ask that no autopsy be done to my body unless required by law. I ask that under no circumstances my body be
turned over for an autopsy, or embalming or for organ donation. I ask that my body be washed, wrapped in cloth
free of any ornaments or articles, prayed for and buried in accordance with Islamic traditions. I ask that all
attempts be made to bury me in a Muslim's cemetery. I ask that my burial take place as soon as possible,
preferably before sunset on the day of my death or the following day, without any undue delay.

I hereby nominate and appoint ___________________________________, to execute these and other necessary
provisions for my proper Islamic funeral and burial. In the event ___________________________ shall be unable
or unwilling to execute, I hereby nominate and appoint ___________________________ to execute these
provisions.

I direct the executor of my funeral and burial rites to follow the instructions in the attached document "Funeral
Guidelines", as well as the following practices at my funeral and burial:
____
____

Article II. EXECUTOR AND GUARDIAN

I hereby nominate and appoint ___________________________ to be the executor of my Will. In the event that
___________________________ predeceases me or shall be unable or unwilling to act as my executor, I nominate
and appoint ___________________________ to act as my executor. I direct that no bond or surety for any bond
be required for my executor in performance of his or her duties.

I give the executor the power to settle any claim for or against my estate, and for this purpose he has the power
to sell, lease, mortgage or otherwise encumber any property, real or personal, that may be included in my estate,
with or without an order of the court, without bond, with due notice to all the heirs.

____
(Testator)

Page 1 of 8

LAST WILL AND TESTAMENT OF

____

[Name of Testator]

I, ____ [Name of Testator], a resident of _____________________, California, being of sound and disposing mind and memory and over the age of eighteen (18) years or lawfully married or having been lawfully married or a member of the armed forces of the United States or a member of an auxiliary of the armed forces of the United States or a member of the maritime service of the United States, and not being actuated by any duress, menace, fraud, mistake, or undue influence, do make, publish, and declare this to be my last Will, hereby expressly revoking all Wills and Codicils previously made by me.

I. MARRIAGE AND CHILDREN

I am married to ____, and all references in this Will to my _________________ [husband or wife] are references to _________________ [him or her]. I have the following children:

Name: _____________________________________ Date of Birth: __________________
Name: _____________________________________ Date of Birth: __________________
Name: _____________________________________ Date of Birth: __________________
Name: _____________________________________ Date of Birth: __________________

II. EXECUTOR: I appoint ____ as Executor of this my Last Will and Testament and provide if this Executor is unable or unwilling to serve then I appoint ____ as alternate Executor. My Executor shall be authorized to carry out all provisions of this Will and pay my just debts, obligations and funeral expenses.

III. GUARDIAN: In the event I shall die as the sole parent of minor children, then I appoint ____ as Guardian of said minor children. If this named Guardian is unable or unwilling to serve, then I appoint ____ as alternate Guardian.

IV. SIMULTANEOUS DEATH OF SPOUSE: In the event that my _________________ [wife or husband] shall die simultaneously with me or there is no direct evidence to establish that my _________________ [wife or husband] and I died other than simultaneously, I direct that I shall be deemed to have survived my _________________ [wife or husband], notwithstanding any provision of law to the contrary, and that the provisions of my Will shall be construed on such presumption.

V. SIMULTANEOUS DEATH OF BENEFICIARY: If any beneficiary of this Will, including any beneficiary of any trust established by this Will, other than my _________________ [wife or husband], shall die within 30 days of my death or prior to he distribution of my estate, I hereby declare that I shall be deemed to have survived such person.

VI. BEQUESTS:

I will, give, and bequeath unto the persons named below, if he or she survives me, the Property described below:

Name: _____________________________________
Address: _____________________________________

____

Name

Personal Plans

Witness 1_______________

Witness 2_______________

These are the instructions for my Advance Directive and Last Will and Testament.

Advance Directive:

Person I Choose as my Health Care Agent: (trust with medical care and services)

1st ____

    Address____

    City/State/Zip ___________________________________

    Phone ____

2nd ____

    Address____

    City/State/Zip ___________________________________

    Phone ____

3rd ____

    Address____

    City/State/Zip ___________________________________

    Phone ____

Physician(s) ____

              ____

              ____

Hospital/Care Facility: ___________________________________

Updates:

____

____

____

____

____

____

____

____

____

____

____

____

____

____

____

____

____

____

____

____

____

____

____

____

Signature_________________________________ Date _____________________

List of Responsibilities of Health Care Agent: (Check all that apply)

___ Make decisions for tests, medication, and surgeries.

___ Make decisions for life saving treatments.

___ Interpret any instructions I have given in this form or any discussions.

concerning my wishes.

___ Consent to the admission to an assisted living, hospital, Nursing Home,

Rehab or Hospice

for me.

___ Interview and hire in home care workers as needed. Also have the authority

to fire and replace in home care workers.

___ Make the decision to request, give or refuse medical treatment, including

artificially provided food and water, and any other treatment to keep me

alive.

___ Review and approve the release of my medical and personal records.

___ Sign medical consents on my behalf.

___ Consent to move me to another state to receive medical care or to carry out

my wishes.

___ Make decisions on medication for pain management.

___ Take any legal actions needed to carry out my wishes.

___ Have access to all records needed to apply for government assistance and

community programs related to my age and health conditions.

Updates:

____

Signature_______________________________ **Date** _______________

Listed below are any changes, limitations, or restrictions of my health Care Agent's power:

____

____

____

____

____

____

____

Things I want and do not want.

Pain Management:

____ I want a second opinion for any diagnosis given for serious.

   illnesses or diseases.

____ I do not want to be in pain. I want the strongest safest medicine available.

____ I can manage some pain. I do not want to be given strong pain medication.

____ I do not want any narcotic pain medication. Non habit forming medication

   only.

____ I want to be offered food and water by mouth if it is safe for me.

____ I want to be kept clean and warm, with daily grooming.

____ I do not want anything done or omitted by doctors or nurses with the

   intention of taking my life.

____ I do want life support measures taken to keep me alive. (Devices for water

   and food, CPR, Transfusions, dialysis, and any other means of keeping me

   alive.

____ I do not want any life support measures done to keep me alive.

Updates:

____
____
____
____
____
____
____
____
____
____
____
____
____
____
____
____
____
____
____
____
____
____
____
____

Signature_______________________________ **Date** _______________________

___ **If in a coma I want life support measures taken.**

___ **If second opinion finds that I am brain dead, totally dependent on oxygen, I do not want life support.**

Other conditions I do not want to be kept alive and will consider Hospice are:

____

____

____

____

____

____

Certain limits and considerations are listed below in my own writing to make it clear that everyone understands my wishes.

____

____

____

____

____

____

____

____

____

____

____

____

____

____ **Do not Resuscitate.**

____ **Resuscitate (3 times)**

____ **Continue Resuscitation**

____ **Only the Health Care Agents listed can make these decisions if I am unable to.**

Updates:

Signature_______________________________________ Date ____________________

_____ My spouse, family members, partner can make decisions if agreed as a majority vote if I am unable to make decisions.

My Last Days

___ I want family and friends around me when possible.

___ I only want certain people around me.

____

____

____

____

____

___ I want to interact with people as much as possible.

___ I want my care givers to what is necessary if I begin to show signs of depression. Become delusional, shortness of breath or nausea.

___ I want my pastor and members of my faith to know of my condition and pray for me.

___ I want my pastor to come pray with me.

___ I want to be cared for with kindness, love, and joy, not sadness.

___ I want a lot of stories of fun times, even if I cannot respond.

___ I want my family to get counseling, if necessary.

___ I want my organs to be donated for research.

___ I do not want my organs to be donated for research.

___ I want to be cremated.

___ I want to be buried in the ground __ Vault__.

I want my body or remains to be placed at:

____

Updates:

Signature_________________________________ Date _____________________

Funeral/ Memorial or Final Rest Arrangements

This is how I want to be remembered:

____

____

____

____

Funeral/Memorial Location

____

____

____ I want a wake service ____ I do not want a wake service.

Flowers:_____________________   **Colors:**_______________________________

Music: _____________________   **Songs**_______________________________

Reading/ Poems: ____

Resolutions: ____

Special Words by family and friends:

____

____

Scriptures: ____

Eulogy: ____

____ I want the viewing of my body before the service and remain closed during

the service.

____ I want the viewing of my body to be done during the service after the
Eulogy.

____ I want my body to be buried at: _________________________________

____ I want my ashes to be released at: _______________________________

____ I want my ashes kept in an urn at this location:___________________

Repast:____

Updates:

____
____
____
____
____
____
____
____
____
____
____
____
____
____
____
____
____
____
____
____
____
____
____
____
____

Signature_______________________________ **Date** _____________________

Last Will and Testament

I have chosen the listed people as my first, second and third executors of my Last Will and Testament. I have also chosen two alternates if all other executors or not available or capable of carrying out my wishes.

1st ________________________________ 2nd ________________________________

3rd ________________________________ Alternate 1st ________________________

Alternate 2nd ________________________

 All of my important documents are in the possession of ________________________

And copies are in the possession of ________________________________ which include insurance information, deeds, and other important information.

Assets and Beneficiary:

____

____

____

____

____

____

____

____

Updates:

____

____

____

____

____

____

____

____

____

____

____

____

____

____

____

____

____

____

____

____

____

____

____

____

____

Signature_________________________________**Date** ____________________________

Residuary Clause covers all assets not listed above. To be distributed by executor in charge. Anything negotiated will be by the so discretion of the executor.

Guardianship of Children: ___________________________________

Guardianship of Pets: ___________________________________

Personal Instructions to be carried out:

____
____
____
____
____
____

Funeral/ Memorial or Final Rest Arrangements

This is how I want to be remembered:

____
____
____
____

Funeral/Memorial Location

____
____

___ I want a wake service ___ I do not want a wake service.

Flowers:___________________ **Colors:**_______________________________

Music: ___________________ **Songs**_______________________________

Reading/ Poems: ____

Resolutions: ____

Updates:

____

____

____

____

____

____

____

____

____

____

____

____

____

____

____

____

____

____

____

____

____

____

____

____

____

____

____

____

Signature_______________________________ **Date** ___________________

Special Words by family and friends:

____

____

Scriptures: _______________________________________

Eulogy: ____

___ I want the viewing of my body before the service and remain closed during

 the service.

___ I want the viewing of my body to be done during the service after the

 Eulogy.

___ I want my body to be buried at: ________________________________

___ I want my ashes to be released at: ______________________________

___ I want my ashes kept in an urn at this location:

____

Repast:____

This Last Will and Testament will be reviewed yearly at my discretion and changed as I see fit.

Signed on this ___day of _________Month and Year ___________.

Witness:_______________________________

Witness: _______________________________

Updates:

____

Signature_____________________________ Date _______________________

Notary Signature Page

In the County of ______________. State of ______________. On this _____ day of ______. ____.

before me. the undersigned Notary Public personally appeared ______________. personally known to me.

proved to me through documentary evidence. or identified by a credible witness to be the person named in the

foregoing. and executed the same.

____

Notary Signature

____

Printed Name

Commission Number ______________

My Commission expires:_______. 20____

Affix seal/stamp as close to
signature as possible.

____

Name

Personal Plans

Witness 1_______________

Witness 2_______________

These are the instructions for my Advance Directive and Last Will and Testament.

Advance Directive:

Person I Choose as my Health Care Agent: (trust with medical care and services)

1st _______________________________________

    Address_______________________________

    City/State/Zip _________________________

    Phone ________________________________

2nd _______________________________________

    Address_______________________________

    City/State/Zip _________________________

    Phone ________________________________

3rd _______________________________________

    Address_______________________________

    City/State/Zip _________________________

    Phone ________________________________

Physician(s) _______________________________________

        ____

        ____

Hospital/Care Facility: _______________________________

Updates:

____
____
____
____
____
____
____
____
____
____
____
____
____
____
____
____
____
____
____
____
____
____
____
____

Signature_______________________________ **Date** _______________________

List of Responsibilities of Health Care Agent: (Check all that apply)

___ Make decisions for tests, medication, and surgeries.

___ Make decisions for life saving treatments.

___ Interpret any instructions I have given in this form or any discussions.

concerning my wishes.

___ Consent to the admission to an assisted living, hospital, Nursing Home,

Rehab or Hospice for me.

___ Interview and hire in home care workers as needed. Also have the authority

to fire and replace in home care workers.

___ Make the decision to request, give or refuse medical treatment, including

artificially provided food and water, and any other treatment to keep me

alive.

___ Review and approve the release of my medical and personal records.

___ Sign medical consents on my behalf.

___ Consent to move me to another state to receive medical care or to carry out

my wishes.

___ Make decisions on medication for pain management.

___ Take any legal actions needed to carry out my wishes.

___ Have access to all records needed to apply for government assistance and

community programs related to my age and health conditions.

Updates:

____

Signature_______________________________ Date ___________________

Listed below are any changes, limitations, or restrictions of my health Care Agent's power/authority:

____

____

____

____

____

____

Things I want and do not want.

Pain Management:

____ I want a second opinion for any diagnosis given for serious.

   illnesses or diseases.

____ I do not want to be in pain. I want the strongest safest medicine available.

____ I can manage some pain. I do not want to be given strong pain medication.

____ I do not want any narcotic pain medication. Non-habit-forming medication.

   only.

____ I want to be offered food and water by mouth if it is safe for me.

____ I want to be kept clean and warm, with daily grooming.

____ I do not want anything done or omitted by doctors or nurses with the

   intention of taking my life.

____ I do want life support measures taken to keep me alive. (Devices for water

   and food, CPR, Transfusions, dialysis, and any other means of keeping me

   alive.

____ I do not want any life support measures done to keep me alive.

____ If in a coma I want life support measures taken.

Updates:

____

____

____

____

____

____

____

____

____

____

____

____

____

____

____

____

____

____

____

____

____

____

____

____

____

____

____

Signature_________________________________ **Date** _____________________

_____ If second opinion finds that I am brain dead, totally dependent on oxygen, I do not want life support.

Other conditions I do not want to be kept alive and will consider Hospice are:

____

____

____

____

____

____

Certain limits and considerations are listed below in my own writing to make it clear that everyone understands my wishes.

____

____

____

____

____

____

____

____

____

____

____

____

____

_____ Do not Resuscitate.

_____ Resuscitate (3 times)

_____ Continue Resuscitation

_____ Only the Health Care Agents listed can make these decisions if I am unable to.

_____ My spouse, family members, partner can make decisions if agreed as a majority vote if I am unable to make decisions.

Updates:

Signature___________________________________ **Date** _____________________

My Last Days

____ I want family and friends around me when possible.

____ I only want certain people around me.

____

____
____
____
____

____ I want to interact with people as much as possible.

____ I want my care givers to what is necessary if I begin to show signs of

depression. Become delusional, shortness of breath or nausea.

____ I want my pastor and members of my faith to know of my condition and

pray for me.

____ I want my pastor to come pray with me.

____ I want to be cared for with kindness, love, and joy, not sadness.

____ I want a lot of stories of fun time, even if I cannot respond.

____ I want my family to get counseling, if necessary.

____ I want my organs to be donated for research.

____ I do not want my organs to be donated for research.

____ I want to be cremated.

____ I want to be buried in the ground __ Vault__.

____ I want my body or remains to be placed at:

____

Updates:

____

Signature_____________________________ Date _____________________

Funeral/ Memorial or Final Rest Arrangements

This is how I want to be remembered:

____

____

____

Funeral/Memorial Location

____

____

___ I want a wake service ___ I do not want a wake service.

Flowers:____________________   Colors:_______________________

Music: _____________________   Songs______________________

Reading/ Poems: ____

Resolutions: ____

Special Words by family and friends:

____

____

Scriptures: ____

Eulogy: ____

___ I want the viewing of my body before the service and remain closed during

   the service.

___ I want the viewing of my body to be done during the service after the

   Eulogy.

___ I want my body to be buried at: ____________________________________

___ I want my ashes to be released at: __________________________________

___ I want my ashes kept in an urn at this location: ______________________

Repast:____

Updates:

____

____

____

____

____

____

____

____

____

____

____

____

____

____

____

____

____

____

____

____

____

____

____

____

Signature_________________________________ **Date** _____________________

Last Will and Testament

I have chosen the listed people as my first, second and third executors of my Last Will and Testament. I have also chosen two alternates if all other executors or not available or capable of carrying out my wishes.

1st _______________________________ 2nd _______________________________

3rd _______________________________ Alternate 1st _______________________

Alternate 2nd _______________________

 All of my important documents are in the possession of _______________________

And copies are in the possession of _______________________________ which include insurance information, deeds, and other important information.

Assets and Beneficiary:

____
____

____
____

____
____

____
____

____

Updates:

____

____

____

____

____

____

____

____

____

____

____

____

____

____

____

____

____

____

____

____

____

____

____

Signature___________________________________ **Date** _____________________

Residuary Clause covers all assets not listed above. To be distributed by executor in charge. Anything negotiated will be by the so discretion of the executor.

Guardianship of Children: _______________________________________

Guardianship of Pets: _______________________________________

Personal Instructions to be carried out:

____
____
____
____
____
____

Funeral/ Memorial or Final Rest Arrangements

This is how I want to be remembered:

____
____
____
____

Funeral/Memorial Location

____
____

___ I want a wake service ___ I do not want a wake service.

Flowers:___________________   **Colors:**_______________________________

Music: ____________________   **Songs**_______________________________

Reading/ Poems: ____

Resolutions: ____

Updates:

____

____

____

____

____

____

____

____

____

____

____

____

____

____

____

____

____

____

____

____

____

____

____

____

____

Signature_________________________________ **Date** ____________________

Special Words by family and friends:

____

____

Scriptures: ____

Eulogy: ____

____ I want the viewing of my body before the service and remain closed during

   the service.

____ I want the viewing of my body to be done during the service after the

   Eulogy.

____ I want my body to be buried at: _________________________________

____ I want my ashes to be released at: _______________________________

____ I want my ashes kept in an urn at this location: _____________________

Repast:____

This Last Will and Testament will be reviewed yearly at my discretion and changed as I see fit.

Signed on this ____day of _________Month and Year ____________.

Witness:__________________________

Witness: __________________________

Updates:

____

Signature__________________________________ **Date** ____________________

Remember Me by Christina Rossetti

Remember me when I am gone away,
Gone far away into the silent land;
When you can no more hold me by the hand,
Nor I half turn to go yet turning stay.
Remember me when no more day by day
You tell me of our future that you planned:
Only remember me; you understand
It will be late to counsel then or pray.

Yet if you should forget me for a while
And afterwards remember, do not grieve:

For if the darkness and corruption leave
A vestige of the thoughts that once I had,
Better by far you should forget and smile
Than that you should remember and be sad.

Remember By Deborah Judge

Remember my life, my smiles, kisses and embraces.

Remember the laughter and joy on mine and everyone's faces.

Remember my life not my death, because my dear family and friends my soul is at rest.

Remember Me by Anthony Dowson

Speak of me as you have always done.
Remember the good times, laughter, and fun.

Share the happy memories we've made.
Do not let them wither or fade.

I'll be with you in the summer's sun
And when the winter's chill has come.

I'll be the voice that whispers in the breeze.
I'm peaceful now, put your mind at ease.

I've rested my eyes and gone to sleep,
But memories we've shared are yours to keep.

Sometimes our final days may be a test,
But remember me when I was at my best.

Although things may not be the same,
Don't be afraid to use my name.

Let your sorrow last for just a while.
Comfort each other and try to smile.

I've lived a life filled with joy and fun.
Live on now, make me proud of what you'll become.

Notary Signature Page

In the County of _______________, State of _______________. On this _____ day of _______, _____, before me. the undersigned Notary Public personally appeared _______________, personally known to me. proved to me through documentary evidence. or identified by a credible witness to be the person named in the foregoing. and executed the same.

____
Notary Signature

____
Printed Name
Commission Number _______________
My Commission expires:_________. 20_____

It is our hope this planner helps you in making difficult decisions. We know this is not an easy topic for families, however we know it is very necessary, to put things in place. We have provided two copies for couples.

We pray for peace, strength and comfort for every family.

With Love,

Yamin /Mobile Prayer Warriors Ministry

Yamin.cre8@gmail.com

MPWIM@yahoo.com

Aging, N. I. (2022, October 21). *Advance Care Planning.* Retrieved from National Institute on Aging: www.nia.nih.gov

aging, N. I. (n.d.). *ADVANCE* .

 (Aging, 2022) (Aging With Dignity, 2021)

(Legalzoom, 2021)